FALKLAND ADVENTURE

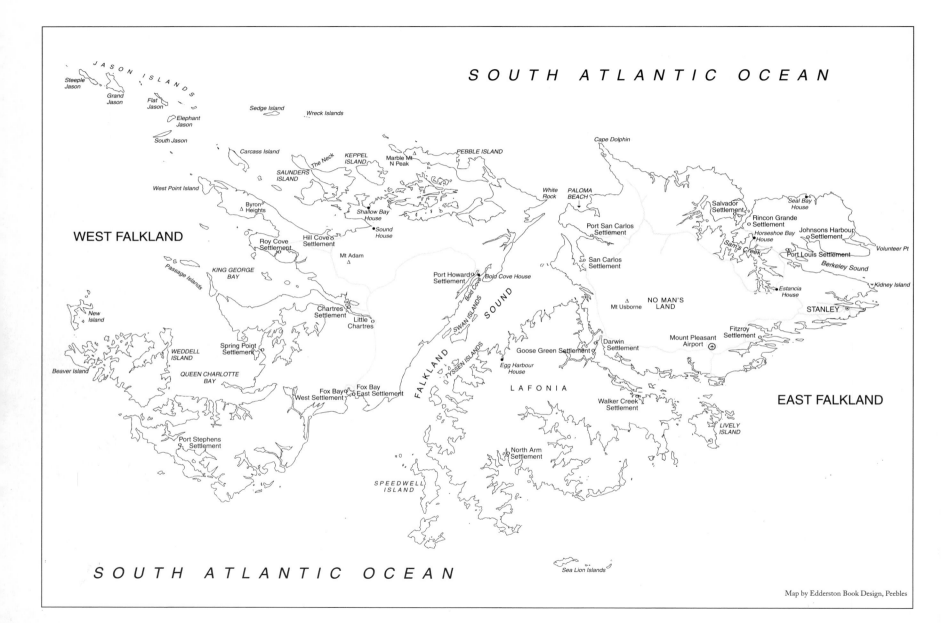

SOUTH ATLANTIC OCEAN

JASON ISLANDS

Steeple Jason
Grand Jason
Flat Jason
Elephant Jason
South Jason

Sedge Island
Wreck Islands

Cape Dolphin

Carcass Island
The Neck
KEPPEL ISLAND
Marble Mt
N Peak
PEBBLE ISLAND

SAUNDERS ISLAND

West Point Island

White Rock
PALOMA BEACH

Salvador Settlement
Seal Bay House
Rincon Grande Settlement
Horseshoe Bay House
Johnsons Harbour Settlement

Byron Heights

Shallow Bay House
Sound House

WEST FALKLAND

Port San Carlos Settlement

Sam's Creek

Port Louis Settlement
Volunteer Pt

Roy Cove Settlement
Hill Cove Settlement

San Carlos Settlement

Berkeley Sound

Mt Adam

KING GEORGE BAY

Port Howard Settlement
Bold Cove House

NO MAN'S LAND

Estancia House
Kidney Island

Passage Islands

Chartres Settlement
Little Chartres

Mt Usborne

STANLEY

New Island

SWAN ISLANDS

FALKLAND SOUND

Fitzroy Settlement

Spring Point Settlement

WEDDELL ISLAND

Darwin Settlement
Mount Pleasant Airport

Goose Green Settlement

Beaver Island

QUEEN CHARLOTTE BAY

TYSSEN ISLANDS

Egg Harbour House

LAFONIA

EAST FALKLAND

Fox Bay West Settlement
Fox Bay East Settlement

Walker Creek Settlement

Port Stephens Settlement

LIVELY ISLAND

North Arm Settlement

SPEEDWELL ISLAND

SOUTH ATLANTIC OCEAN

Sea Lion Islands

Map by Edderston Book Design, Peebles

FALKLAND ADVENTURE

Andrew Coe

Bluebell Publishing, Strathaven

First Published in Great Britain in 2000 by

Bluebell Publishing
Strathaven
Lanarkshire, ML10 6PN

e-mail: bluebell@ukgateway.net

ISBN 0-9538220-1-X

A CIP catalogue record for this book is
available from the British Library

Page i: South American tern
Page iii: Bluebell follows 'The Red Peril'
in the evening sun, heading towards
Paloma Beach, East Falkland

Printed in Great Britain by Bath Press, Glasgow

CONTENTS

INTRODUCTION

The Falkland Islands is a land of mystery, a land that defies definition, full of surprises and a stirrer of mixed and powerful emotions. A stark, bare landscape, dreary at first but which with time, gets beneath your skin, into your heart and mind, and yes, into your soul itself. There is a clarity of light and colour, a serenity of the spirit, and a peace and beauty that reaches inside you, and once there will remain with you for eternity.

I am not a Falkland Islander, and I could not live there forever. But each and every day I think of the land, the people, the wildlife, and of the most amazing experiences that we had in that place. The children amongst penguins, Elephant seals, King cormorants and albatross; fishing in the creeks and rivers; beach-combing on the white sand beaches. I think of camping in the remote and wild places with huge driftwood campfires and the peaceful braying of penguins as we lay in the warmth and snugness of our sleeping bags. Driving through peat bogs, over ditches, and along deserted beaches in our ever faithful Land Rover 'Bluebell'.

I remember the sweet, overpowering smell of the gorse in spring, the azure blue skies on crisp winter days, and the pounding white surf out of a green black sea when the wind blows with a vengeance. The dorsal fins of the Peale's and Commerson's dolphins breaking the water by the kelp beds, the magical drumming and hooting of the Logger ducks who paddle the seas with such poise and grace, and the stark power and malice of a hunting sea lion.

This book is a very personal record of the Falklands, of the way it was to me and my wife Sarah and our five young children, during the three years that we lived there when I worked for the Government as the Senior Veterinary Officer. I hope, through the pictures and words which follow, that some of you at least may be encouraged to take the plunge and make the long trip south, as you set off on the journey to a Falkland adventure of your very own.

Seascape, Cape Dolphin

SEA LION ISLAND

To the south of East Falkland, Sea Lion Island is buffeted by the waves and storms of the South Atlantic. A flat and superficially barren island, initially uninspiring but one of the 'must see' places in this incredible archipelago. It is here that you can most easily see more variety of wildlife in a shorter space of time, than anywhere else in the Falklands.

Visit in October/early November to see the newborn black and velvet smooth Elephant seal pups, and the huge bulls protecting their harems. At this time too the Gentoo, Magellanic and Rockhopper penguins will be preparing their nests and sitting on eggs, as will the myriad of smaller birds such as Rufous-chested dotterels and Two-banded plovers.

Later on in December and January, the Southern sea lions are ashore and their active and vocal pups will be clambering around the rocks at the water's edge, trying desperately to avoid being crushed by the scaringly powerful and fast moving dominant bulls. By now, penguin chicks and goslings will be there in abundance, and the King cormorants and Rock shags too will have their young on display. If you are lucky you will see a pod of Killer whales, patrolling only thirty or forty metres off the beach, on the prowl for sea lions, Elephant seals and penguins. The Elephants seals will be there still, now more relaxed, the mating over, with rival males happy to lie together side by side in laddish bliss.

It is about a twenty-five minute flight from Stanley to Sea Lion. Our family arrived en masse early one Saturday morning in November. A family of seven takes up quite a bit of a ten seater Islander plane and the only other passenger, Bill, an Ear, Nose and Throat Consultant from Scotland kindly lent a hand with chaperoning the kids. We landed at the western end of the island on the old grass strip, (there is now a new clay strip right next to the lodge), and Dave Gray, a Yorkshireman with a great enthusiasm for the wildlife and the then owner of Sea Lion Lodge, met us in his Land Rover. Striated caracaras (Johnny Rooks), some of the rarest birds of prey in the world, perched on the plane's wings and tail whilst we unloaded our luggage.

On the trip to the lodge Dave kept us all fully occupied by pointing out the Bumble bee like dotterel chicks hiding in the long grass; the Silver teal and Chiloe wigeon on the great pond; and the Crested caracara, perched watching us on a Diddle-dee bog on the brow of a rise. He was patience itself, and when later that afternoon he took us on a tour of the island he baby-sat the kids so that Sarah and I could peer over sheer cliffs, and lent them his binoculars to watch the ducks and geese on the ponds.

The children were in awe of and not a little frightened by the Elephant seals with their huge bulk and burping sounds; amused and

Large bull Elephant seal relaxing on the beach

1

entertained by the nest stealing antics of the penguins; and Joe fell in love with the little brown Tussac birds which came and perched on his feet and took crumbs from his hand. Dave and his wife Pat helped make our stay a wonderful memory and when we all returned a little over a year later, this time in January, we were lucky enough to see Killer whales on several occasions close in to the shore as they cruised around the kelp beds.

Bull Elephant seal close up

Left. Gentoo penguin. Above. Cow Elephant seal 'burps' a warning

Magellanic oystercatchers

Common (Magellan) snipe

Female Kelp goose at rest

The big Elephant came out of the sea and roared his challenge. The master bull raised his head from where he lay in the centre of the harem, and, throwing his head and tail alternatively backwards and forwards, he pivoted round to point in the direction of the newcomer. With a wave like motion rippling down the blubber of his eighteen foot long body he crashed his way through the melee of cows and calves that scattered from his path. The challenger was more bluff than substance and with no stomach for a fight melted back into the surf without so much as throwing a punch.

At the edge of the beach where the waves broke onto the shore, halfway between two separate and well claimed harems, a pair of young Elephant bulls sparred. There was no malice or urgency in their fight, it was more the good-natured jostling of a couple of adolescent lads in the dinner queue.

They reared up and clashed with their chests and necks but the thrusts with their bared teeth were deliberately half hearted. The whole charade lasted for ten or fifteen minutes and then they lay down together nose to nose and let the cooling of the waves wash over them.

Elephant seals mating at the water's edge

On top of the cliff the air whirred with the wing beats of King cormorants as they flew in from the fishing grounds to feed their chicks. Rockhopper penguins were interspersed amongst them, yellow eye tassels streaming in the wind. Whilst Sarah grappled to keep the children back from the crumbling edge, I followed Dave down a steep rocky path up which the 'Rockies' were constantly struggling.

We rounded a corner and came across a pair of Dolphin gulls, cuddled up together like lovers on a park bench. Their heads and necks were of delicate smoke, their beaks of pillar-box red. The gusting wind ruffled their feathers as they snuggled close for comfort. It was pure romance and we quietly left them to each other's company.

This time I had come to Sea Lion to do a job of work, to castrate a couple of calves, and do some routine testing on the milk cows. Once that was finished I had a whole afternoon and evening free, the plane would not be back to fetch me until the morrow.

I wandered across to the beach where the tussac grass grew thick and lush. I lay down on the ice cold sand and dozed in the sun, stirring occasionally to watch the penguins and an errant Elephant seal playing in the shallows. And once when I glanced up, the huge and ominous black dorsal fin of a lone bull Killer whale sailed past like a devilish wind surfer.

In late afternoon I strolled around the point, photographing some Logger ducks on the way, and then came upon a vast number of South American terns and Brown-hooded gulls resting on the shore. They took to the air and all around me was the sight and sound of them, a moving, changing kaleidoscope against a blue background.

Female Logger duck calling

Logger duck with ducklings

I came upon a white sand desert,
Screaming gulls and terns in blue white flight,
Glistening sun in their feathers,
And angels in their wings.

They screamed and danced in gentle motion,
Gleaming, dazzling, piercing shards of living glass.
I could not imagine, nor invent this perfect life,
No other there to share such joy and yet such sadness in my solitary state.

Pastel shades of pink and mauve

Towards dusk I returned to the beach to see it in the splendour of the evening light. Pastel shades of pink and mauve, and later of yellow and gold. The evening sounds of ducks and penguins dusted everything with magic from another world.

EAST FALKLAND

On East Falkland, most of the wildlife and general interest sites can be reached within a three hour drive from Stanley. Although there are made-up roads to a lot of them, you still need a four wheel drive vehicle to reach the best and of course to explore off the beaten track. Historically that always meant a Land Rover or 'Rover' as they are known, (there must be more Land Rovers per head of population in the Falklands than anywhere else in the world), but nowadays Mitsubishis seem equally at home.

If you are a visitor to Stanley there are plenty of tour operators who will take you on a day trip, but if you live there, you've got to get yourself the right vehicle. In our case that meant an old Long Wheel Base Series III Rover with a rusted and holed chassis, and bodywork painted in bright blue gloss paint. We called her 'Bluebell' and she became our friend and companion over the next few years, taking us all over the Falklands. When we left we sent her by ship to Punta Arenas, southern Chile, and drove through Chile and Argentina to Brazil, crossing the Andes in her five times. She now sits quietly in our drive in Scotland, a well deserved retirement.

Nearly every other weekend we would set off from Stanley in Bluebell, heading away from civilisation and out into the unknown, often with our tents and sleeping bags for an overnight stay. Sometimes we would go with friends, but more often we would head away by ourselves, to Rincon Grande, Cape Dolphin, Estancia, Sam's Creek or Volunteers. Even now the names fill me with excitement and once out in 'camp' (away from Stanley), freedom for the kids was absolute.

The mountains of East
Falkland from the air

Huge stone run on the Port Louis road

Heading towards Port Louis, and before you reach the fork where you turn left for Port San Carlos, the track passes through the middle of a mighty stone run, a great snaking river of grey, lichen covered rocks and boulders of all shapes and sizes. No one knows the true origin of them but the best guess is that they were deposited by glaciers many years ago.

Beyond the stone run, as you crest the brow of a hill you will come upon one of my favourite East Falkland views. Seated on the edge of a huge sea water inlet with the hills beyond the Malo river shimmering in the background is Estancia, home of Tony and Ailsa Heathman. On a calm summer's day the waters of the creek are mirror sharp, the colours are as an artist's palette and the air is bright and clear.

There has been many a happy evening fishing for Sea trout from Tony's land at the 'Tar Barrel', in good weather and in bad. I remember one harshly cold and windy night staying on 'till nearly dark and then getting the Government Rover stuck on both offside wheels in a deep, water filled 'Buffalo' ditch. I tried to jack it up, I tried the electric winch but I lacked experience then, and the wind driven sleet chilled me and scared me making me run all the way to Tony and Ailsa's, panting hard. They greeted me with much glee and mock chastisement and warmed me up with hot coffee and a plate of home baking. Then Tony took me in his commandeered ex-Argentine lorry back to my Rover and with a chain round the bumper soon had me pulled out and on my way.

Estancia farm with the Malo hills behind

Keeping warm on our first camp at Horseshoe Bay

It was our first night's camping and not yet having a Land Rover, we'd driven in our car as far as we could in the direction of Rincon Grande farm. We pitched our tents on a green patch of grass just back from the high tide mark and spent the afternoon with the kids gathering all the driftwood we could find. That night we made a fine campfire, and, worried about the twins stumbling into it, we strapped them into their car seats and sat them at a 'light braising' distance from the roaring flames. We sang campfire songs and, as dusk slowly crept in, small flocks of teal and Upland geese winged their way past, coming and going from the feeding grounds.

We put the children to bed and Sarah and I huddled round the fire drinking copious quantities of Chilean red until all the wood had been burnt and the embers glowed deep crimson. We both felt very happy to be there.

The next morning we rekindled the flames and ate a hearty breakfast during which Joe announced completely unprompted, 'This is great!' After washing up in the sea we walked to where a little creek flowed into the ocean. There we caught half a dozen good-sized mullet, which our friends at Foam Creek barbecued for our lunch.

Family of Upland geese

Between Berkeley Sound and Horseshoe Bay there is a little creek that runs into the sea at a place called Dan's Shanty. We named it Sam's Creek. We found it just by chance, out looking one day for a place to fish. We had three brand new and tiny fishing rods and, with eager anticipation, we baited our hooks with scraps of mutton and cast out three lines into the teeth of a howling gale and intermittent sleet showers. Within five minutes we had two, one and a half pound mullet on the bank and the three older boys' hands were red and blue with the beginnings of frost-bite. We decided to call it a day.

We went back again a few weeks later with our friend Crispin and his family; the weather was kinder, and Sam, only four years old was more excited than I had ever seen him. Fishing it seemed, was already his overriding love. The older boys fished for a while, but soon grew bored and ran off to play football and fly kites. Sam, Crispin and I settled down in anticipation of a long wait. To our delight we soon had three mullet hooked and landed, good eating fish, two to three pounds in weight and clean and silvery. And then Sam hooked into his.

I could see immediately that it was a big fish by the way the float dragged right under and the tip of the rod bent down to point straight into the water. Sam squealed and I rushed over to help him steady it. Back and forth went the fish, it was a simple, cheap reel and I had to keep adjusting the drag on the line to stop it being too slack or worse still, snapping with the force of a sudden jerk. Slowly, slowly we worked the mullet nearer the beach.

A jagged dorsal fin broke the surface, its belly flashed white and then we felt the power and pull on the line as it headed back out to sea on a dash to escape. Sam's little face was a picture of concentration as he played it, again bringing it closer to the shore and again seeing it make a run but perhaps weaker now. In all, it took about ten minutes to get it ashore, the size of it was staggering and the other kids rushed over for a look whilst Sam wore a smile and expression that was a mixture of pride and embarrassment.

When we got home we weighed it with a spring balance. It was exactly ten pounds. Sam had landed perhaps the biggest fish he would ever catch in his life. Over the next three years we spent many happy days fishing at Sam's Creek; it is a passion that has never left him.

Esme catches a 4lb mullet at Sam's Creek

Everyone in Stanley was talking about them, the great whales crowded into Berkeley Sound, presumably attracted by the krill that had drifted in on the current. It was many years since so many had been seen in Falkland waters.

With luck and excitement we persuaded a neighbour, David McLeod to take us out in his small boat one Saturday morning to try and get a glimpse of them. We left the twins with a friend and Sarah and I, Joe, James and Sam set off with David, through 'The Narrows' at the entrance to Stanley Harbour, and then out past Sparrow Cove and towards Kidney Island. Commerson's dolphins raced to join us and play in the bow wave, coming so close we could have leant over and touched them.

Past Kidney Island we saw our first 'blow', a huge plume of spray shooting ten or even fifteen feet into the air, quickly followed by a smaller, fatter one close by. David cut the engine and we drifted over towards them as the strong smell of krill laced whale breath engulfed the boat and then passed on like a poisonous cloud. Sixty feet away another huge blow and then a great whale surfaced, its huge flat head with a central ridge running towards the snout, plain to see. It stayed on the surface for a few seconds, another two smaller ones joined it and then they slowly dived, the small dorsal fin of each of them eventually breaking the surface and then disappearing in a sweeping arc.

We headed further in to Berkeley Sound and spent an hour drifting on the tide, drinking coffee from a flask and eating sandwiches, as all around us the sight and smell of the 'blows' of tens of Sei and Fin whales rose like a fountain display into the air.

Commerson's dolphin riding along beside our boat

Above. Bluebell and our camp at Cape Dolphin
Below. Family of Southern sea lions

We pitched our tents next to a penguin path behind the dunes, fifty metres from the sea on an expansive coastal green. We overlooked a shallow freshwater lake teeming with water-fowl, a pair of Black-necked swans with four cygnets were a rare treat. This was Cape Dolphin, wild and isolated, my heart stirs even now with the memory.

Leaving our camp, (no fear of thieves here), we drove Bluebell to the eastern side of the cape, up a steep slope, and parked her a few yards from the summit. From here I edged towards the cliff face and peered down over the tussac grass. Below on the damp rock beach, a group of fifty or so adult sea lions with twenty or thirty young pups lay sprawled on the stony shore. Awesome white waves came pounding in over the rocks setting the kelp waving and rocking with each ebb and flow of the grey green water.

Halfway down the sandy bank I saw a huge bull sea lion, golden maned, with tiny, pig like eyes, carefully watching me. He was surrounded by giant tussac bogs and he'd flattened out the grass between them with his great weight and spreading flippers. He was like an animal from a different continent, halfway between Lion and Gorilla in his bulk and demeanour. Right below him, another massive bull stood guard on the beach over his harem of seven or eight cows, and every twenty or thirty metres there was a similar group, each protected by its own bull. On the periphery were the challengers, the masters of tomorrow, some high above in the tussac like my watching friend; others on the edge of the sea ready to take to the water if another bull rushed at them.

Above the rumble of the sea came the intermittent barking call of the cows and the yapping of the smooth black pups who played together like a litter of puppies, chasing, and fighting. One at a time I brought the kids to the edge so that they could see for themselves, and one at a time it put a huge grin on their faces. Then, I crept down the sandy cliff face for a closer look, all too aware of the danger of stumbling on a sleeping 'Lion', indeed I passed a couple of fish smelling and flattened resting places as I made my way down. A couple of Turkey vultures cruised forty or fifty feet above my head, watching for discarded afterbirths or perhaps a dead pup.

Suddenly, I spotted the smooth black outline of a swimming sea lion, an almost full grown bull, anxious to win some cows of his own but not yet with the confidence and desire to press the challenge home. He came to where the sea boiled with foam, perhaps fifteen metres from where I sat, and inclined his head in the sort of way a dog does when it wants your undivided attention. The sea splashed all around him, the foam blew in the wind, and he looked like some prima donna in a foam bath waiting for someone to massage his back and ego.

Above. Cow sea lion suckling her pup
Below. Prima donna in a foam bath

Driving to our fishing place, on a gentle, still day with burning sun, we passed a small pond with Yellow-billed teal and Chiloe wigeon. Suddenly, a smaller bird swam out from the bank, the children focused their binoculars and Joe, the ornithologist, quickly found it in the bird book; a White-tufted grebe. It made its way to the centre of the pond, the surface flat and shiny as fresh satin save for the spreading ripples that followed it along.

Adult Rockhopper penguins on a cliff's edge

King cormorants at Egg Harbour, Lafonia

Rockhopper nursery, Seal bay, East Falkland

Low cloud over Port Salvador, East Falkland

Light on blue and black and gold,
Magic in your eye so bold,
With darting beak and whirr of wing,
You sit and gaze, in truth a King.

The darkening clouds around you grow,
Yet what you think we cannot know,
Your life not touched by human hand,
This place you live, by rights your land.

The future is unsure I feel,
The smell and thrill of oil is real,
These sparkling, clear and raging seas,
A danger lurks and fills the breeze.

For how much longer will this stay,
In peace and beauty day by day,
I hope forever, King of gems
From nature's womb, true beauty stems.

The wind blew cold, about fifteen knots, a mere breeze and already I felt frozen. The colt eyed us with a wild, unfriendly look. He was three years old and well grown, heavily and powerfully muscled, untamed. He trotted round the corral, legs extended, tail and mane flying behind, his eyes spoke murder and the veins in his neck filled and twitched. This would be no easy castration, he was King here and he knew it.

A lasso was thrown over his head and a couple of turns made round a post in the middle of the corral. He reared and plunged and threw himself down in rampant fury. With difficulty I got the anaesthetic into his jugular vein and in a few minutes we had him, this heaving, fuming beast. We rolled him onto his back and, unsure of how long he would stay asleep, I asked John Willy to tie his four legs tight together. It was just as well. A few seconds before the last clamp was due off he awoke and the sudden tensing of his muscles strained his bonds to their limit. I whipped off the clamp, undid the ropes and he rose to his feet in one swift movement, thunder and lightning in his thoughts.

VOLUNTEER POINT

At the eastern most tip of East Falkland, a place called Volunteer Point, there is a breeding colony of several hundred King penguins. They are a two hour 'camp' drive from the nearest made up road at Port Louis, through peat bogs deep enough to lose a Rover in; across overgrown ditches with crumbling sides and hidden rocks; and past the dreaded and disguised 'blue clay' on the beaches. Getting there is an adventure in itself, so go, take your tent and stove; some steaks and a box of Chilean red, and spend a night out there with the Kings. Marvel at their vivid colours; metallic sheens of reflected light; and smile at their human mannerisms and antics.

You will feel as though you are at the end of the earth but it is a good feeling, not a harrowing one since it is shared with the thousands of other penguins and sea birds that thrive there. If you are lucky you will see sea lions and dolphins too.

Opposite. King penguins, Volunteer Point

Left. Courting Kings

With five children and four adults crammed into Bluebell, plus all our camping gear and extra petrol on the roof rack, we had a fair old weight on board. Skirting along the beach I could choose between heading back onto the grass or passing through a small puddle and staying on the shore. Sarah wisely advised the former and I gaily chose the latter.

The front wheel went down into the blue clay with a bump but our momentum bounced it back out. With most of the weight over the rear axle, the offside rear wheel dropped with a metallic crash and stopped us dead in our proverbial tracks. Bluebell tilted sideways, threatened to roll onto her side, then teetered to an undignified halt, the driver's door touching the sand and the near side front wheel suspended eighteen inches in the air.

'Don't move', I said, as if anyone could with most of the luggage now piled on top of them.

One by one, the passengers and then I climbed out of the only available door, lightly shaken perhaps, but certainly not stirred. The kids at once thought it was a great laugh and very quickly so did the adults. On the two-metre radio set I gave a call to Jenny Smith at Johnson's Harbour and within half an hour she came racing over the hill in her Rover, bristling with chunky wide tyres. She towed us out with a chain and a smile, and, apart from a bent and split rear body panel, Bluebell was happily none-the-worse for the experience and raring to go again.

King penguin displaying

Bluebell, three wheels on the ground!

'Let me whisper in your ear'   It was a privilege indeed to camp just a couple of hundred yards from the King penguin colony and to be able to go and visit them whenever we wanted. We ate our supper to the sound of their haunting calls, lay down to sleep beneath their calming cries, and awoke to the tune of their dawn chorus. As we cooked egg and bacon for breakfast, they wandered past us on their way to the sea, pausing every now and then to glance around them and sometimes to observe us with a seemingly more than passing interest.

Time and again we wandered up just to be in their presence; to watch their swaggering stilted gait; their loafing around in groups as though on street corners; and the strengthening of the bond between breeding pairs with outstretched hooting, gentle bill fencing, and intimate 'whispering' of one to the other. Those already with eggs stood in hunched silence, the solitary egg balanced carefully on their flippered feet and covered by a feathered abdominal fold to keep it warm.

On the beach itself, a large group of Gentoos gathered at the water's edge, paddling and playing in the breaking waves, a watchful eye out for marauding sea lions. A hunting Peregrine passed along the dunes, a dark, ominous, arrow-headed shape, fleet of wing and sharp of eye and beak. Dotterels and plovers sounded their alarm and shrank down onto the sand. This was nature in the raw, unmanaged and untouched, just as had been intended.

You look at me,
I look at you,
And who can say which is the fool,

You sitting there,
Me standing here,
Which one it is just isn't clear.

You think you're smart,
I think you're dumb,
And I am not the only one.

You smile at me,
I laugh at you,
'cos I can see you've trod in poo.

PEBBLE ISLAND

We arrived at Pebble Island for a weekend break at Pebble Lodge to celebrate Sam's seventh birthday. Long and narrow off the northern coast of West Falkland its three mountain peak landmarks can be seen for miles around on a good clear day. On the way we had skimmed the West Falkland coastline, passing over White Rock and then flying low past a rocky islet covered in sea lions who seemed to rear up threateningly and look through the windows at us we were so close.

Now our little plane wheeled round and came in for its final run. Looking through the windscreen I could see the waves breaking onto the sandy beach left damp by the retreating tide. Parked near the dunes was Pebble Lodge's Rover and, on a moveable pole, a bright orange windsock flapped horizontally in the strong wind.

A mass of gulls and small waders was on the shoreline feeding on the creatures stirred up by the waves. A sharp gust of wind caused our wings to wobble but Morgan the pilot corrected it with a flick of the joystick. The crosswind was so strong we were pointed at an almost forty-five degree angle to the beach landing strip which became more and more obvious as we got nearer and nearer to the ground. At the last second Morgan straightened the fuselage and dropped us ever so gently onto the sand, a remarkable feat of flying.

The gulls and oystercatchers took flight as we sped past them, bouncing over patches of kelp strewn across the shore. A penguin making his way up the beach took one look at us, turned, and headed back to the sanctuary of the icy waters on his belly, legs and flippers going flat out.

'Welcome to Pebble Island' said Morgan, turning to me with a smile.

Islander aircraft landing on
Pebble Island beach

Above. Rockhopper penguin
Below. Salt spray on our faces

James, the Lodge manager, had dropped us at the pebble beach and we'd spent some time hunting for the precious stones that give the island its name. Now, as we walked from Marble Shanty across the far western peninsula to the north coast, we were weighed down with jangling pockets of coloured rocks. Twenty or so of Raymond Evans' horses galloped over to see us, nostrils dilated with excitement, kicking up their heals and squealing with false frenzy. We ushered the kids into close formation as they circled round us, more curious than aggressive but a stray kick could maim or even kill. Eventually they decided they'd seen enough and, taking mock fright, they galloped off again over towards the sand grass dunes.

Sarah and Nat climbed to the top of Marble Mountain from where they could look back the ten or so miles to the settlement. The rest of us made our way round the bottom edge, picking our way past the penguin burrows and rocky crags. Along the cliff edge, the first of the Rockhoppers had returned, power-packed little bundles of energy that somehow survived the ocean's relentless might.

The wind was still blowing strong, directly off the sea which was a rich deep blue and green in the bright sunlight. White-topped waves broke with force onto the jagged rocks and we all climbed down onto them to feel the ice salt spray on our faces.

We travelled back to the lodge across a beach and then up the side of a steep dune. Gentoos on the way to their nest site struggled up in front of us, walking with a sense of purpose that was almost inspirational. Even more impressive was the huge number of Giant Petrels or 'Stinkers' who were taking advantage of the wind and air currents to swoop down at the hill face and then, catching the updraft, rise like rockets to clear the hump and speed on over the other side.

SAUNDERS ISLAND

My first trip to Saunders Island was to see a horse with chronic grass sickness. I was met at the plane by Dave Pole-Evans, the archetypal larger than life character. He is a big man physically, as strong as an ox, and with a sarcasm that matches my own. He and his wife Sue farm Saunders, the second largest of the outer Islands, a great sweeping horseshoe with high mountains, secluded bays, and several miles of rocky, tussac strewn cliffs. They run about ten thousand sheep but like most farmers are probably finding the present economics of farming sheep for their wool pretty dismal. Increasingly, tourism is playing its part in helping them to make ends meet. The great wildlife attractions of Saunders are the huge colonies of Black-browed albatross, Rockhopper and Gentoo penguins, King cormorants, and a small breeding colony of King penguins.

In the afternoon, Dave took me to the north coast to see some albatross. It was the start of the nesting season and the birds were pairing up, anxious to claim their own little bit of territory around their raised mud nest. The air was filled with their soaring flight, hardly a beat of the wing, just a powerful, cutting glide with a steady forward gaze. Time and again a bird would come in to the cliff as if to land, veer off at the last moment, and then, with a huge sweeping circle against the wind come around for another try.

What struck me was the total lack of fear in the birds and their huge size. I sat just a few feet away from them and they were completely unperturbed. Their courtship was tenderness itself, the stroking and clicking of beaks; neck and chin preening; and simply sitting together in close contact. The sharp contrast in their plumage of purest white against deepest black gave them an almost reverential glow. No person could possibly design a creature such as this.

The great horseshoe-shaped
Saunders Island in evening
light

Above left. Black-browed albatross

Above. Courtship behaviour

Left. Preening keeps the feathers in good condition

Right. Pure beauty

Watching the air show

I returned to Saunders a few weeks later with Sarah and the kids at the start of a week long West Isles tour. Dave and Sue took us up to 'The Neck', a narrow isthmus of land that is the prime wildlife site on the Island. In just a couple of hours you can have your fill of four species of penguin, Magellanic; Gentoo; Rockhopper; and King, (sometimes with a Macaroni or even a Chinstrap thrown in); Black-browed albatross; King cormorants, and Rock shags. No wonder people come from all the world to visit, and here was I, for the most part, being paid for it.

It was a glorious spring day. The sun shone down fiercely and we lay on our backs on the green grass slope facing out to sea, watching the albatross glide silently overhead.

Saunders Island Kings at 'The Neck'

Rockhopper penguin

WEST POINT ISLAND

I had been trying for nearly two years to visit West Point Island, a small, almost subtropical paradise just off the western tip of West Falkland. I needed to sample Lily's milk cows and as each appointment came closer, Roddy Napier would phone and cancel, either citing the landing strip as being too wet or that the forecast was bad and I was bound to be stranded for days. I began to think he didn't want me to go! Now that I had eventually arrived, I think he thought I wasn't quite so bad after all, especially as the sampling had passed without injury to man or beast. Roddy and his wife Lily were kindness itself.

After lunch he took me down to the bay to see the old shearing shed and to our surprise we saw a bright blue and white yacht heading for the beach. It was Bernard Betts from The Boundary farm, Hill Cove, enjoying a day out on the water. He came ashore and helped me trim the hooves of one of Roddy's old white ponies and then stayed for tea. When he left, the tide was right out and there were dozens of Kelp geese feeding amongst the bright emerald green seaweed that lay rich and thick like a late spring field of grass.

Immature Kelp geese
foraging at low tide

Hung above the door of the old shearing shed is the largest sea lion skull you will ever see. Covered in lichens and with some of the dried skin still remaining, its lifeless grimace is a stark testament to the savage destruction of the Southern sea lion population earlier this century and right up to the 1960's. For the purpose of boiling them up for oil, their numbers were reduced from several hundred thousands to just a few thousands. Now, in more enlightened times, no one kills sea lions in the Falklands. Indeed all Falkland Islanders seem only too aware of the importance of safeguarding the wildlife and ecology of their land for the future, and the organisation Falklands Conservation appears to be going from strength to strength. With luck and hard work the sea lions may recover, a great step forward for the Falklands and the world as a whole.

Islander circling in the bay

The Islander did one pass and then headed out to the freedom of the bay where it circled for a few minutes whilst Roddy chased the wild geese from the airstrip with his old Rover. The Johnny Rooks lined up on the fence posts and Lily kept them occupied with lumps of mutton. FIGAS pilot Troyd was on a training flight and we watched as he did four near perfect touchdowns on the short, 380 metre strip, each time accelerating immediately to lift off again and clear the boundary fence. The skill and professionalism of all the pilots and the confidence that I had in them to get us safely home in all weathers, is something that lingers in my memory. I understand but do not share the average military person's name for FIGAS of 'White Knuckle Airways'.

Young Black-browed albatross on the point of fledging

WEST FALKLAND

There is a popular saying on West Falkland that 'West is best', and after working and holidaying amongst this ever dwindling band of stoical pioneers I have to say that I agree. For me, West Falkland is more beautiful, more remote, more traditional and more enthralling than the East. I hope you Easters will forgive me for saying so.

In the first place, you can only reach the West by boat or plane so the Westers have a more self-contained and independent view of life. And whilst Easters are hospitable, the real Wester has more of what I imagine is that 'old camp hospitality' of welcoming total strangers into their home for 'smoko', dinner, or even a bed for the night. This hospitality surfaces no more obviously than at the annual camp sports.

Every year in late February when all the shearing is finished, or at least nearly so, the camp sports come around, a week of celebration and dancing; horse racing; sheep dog trials; sheep shearing competitions, and golf. The West has its version and the East has its, and two years running we loaded Bluebell onto the coastal vessel 'Tamar' and shipped her over to the West for the week. Oh for such bliss again.

The first year we spent a day fishing in the Chartres river in glorious sunshine. The three older boys all caught their first Sea trout, which we filleted and fried in butter and black pepper there and then on the bankside, the rich pinky orange fillets almost melting in our mouths. We camped the night at Little Chartres and Tony and Lynn Blake invited us in for a huge roast lamb supper washed down with Chilean 'Gato Negro'.

The next day we drove to the sports themselves, that year at Hill Cove settlement, Bluebell taking us in pouring rain up and over the treacherous mountain track known as 'Hell's Kitchen'. Her tyres were really too bald for these conditions and as we crossed one particularly tricky ditch the steep muddy bank beyond defeated us and we slipped sideways almost into the ditch itself. There was no grip to be had and then Sarah had the brainwave of pulling a mass of dried Diddle-dee bush which we laid under all four wheels and for several yards in front. With traction restored and in low ratio four wheel drive we were up and away. Huge boulders rattled against the chassis, we bounced and eased our way along, and the rain leaked in through the doors and splashed up through the holes in the floor panels as we ploughed through deep puddles. We stayed in the 'big house' with Tim and Sally Blake who could not have been kinder or more generous hosts, and treated the kids like surrogate grandchildren.

The second year we drove to Tim and Sally's 'Sound House', an old shepherds hut with no electricity, only Tilley lamps and a Kerosene heater. We spent three of our happiest days there in complete isolation, fishing for Sea trout and hunting for whale and bird skulls

The view of Saunders Island from 'the big house', Hill Cove

Above. Jockeys and horses, Hill Cove sports
Below. Bluebell being loaded onto the Tamar for the crossing to West Falkland

and shells along the beach. When we left we headed to Jimmy and Ginny Forster's at Bold Cove, across the bay from Port Howard, the most relaxing of places for Sarah, as Ginny is so calm and straightforward with the kids.

From their kitchen/dining-room you look through a big picture window, down the harbour towards the setting sun, and can watch the Islanders arriving and leaving with their cargo of camp sports revellers. As Jimmy has said to me on more than one occasion, 'Why would I want to change all this?' I can only agree with him.

On Saturday afternoon we walked to the top of the ridge behind the house, the kids scrambled amongst the rocky crags and the wind blew their coats and stung their cheeks. At the summit it seemed like we were at the top of the world, Everest must be like this only many times more so. A Red-backed hawk glided by in silence only yards away from where we sat and some minutes later, in violent contrast, we looked down on two RAF Tornados screaming up the valley with fire and great noise in their wake.

Above. On the ridge above Bold Cove
Right. Joe by the Chartres river with his first Sea trout

At Spring Point farm, Ron and Fiona Rozee live the Falkland dream. A farm and golf course of their own, some good land, and their own string of horses that they train for the camp sports. It is idyllic but lonely as well, it takes a special sort of person to make a go of it once the romanticism has worn off and the two of them fit that bill.

We flew out to stay with them one Easter, the weather was fine and they minded the kids for us whilst Sarah and I went for a two hour horse ride along the coast. The riding style is South American with a fleece or two on top of the saddle and the horses controlled largely by neck reining. It is both comfortable and relaxing.

In the afternoon Ron cooked up a barbecue in the front garden using driftwood collected from the beaches. He grilled a mountain of mutton chops, thick and fat laden, Falklands style. Sam rose to the occasion, chewing his way through five of them, a broad smile on his face and thick grease on his chin. Later, as the sun turned orange we took an inflatable dinghy down to the shore and rowed to and from Fox Island as the tide slowly made its way up the creek. Then the children helped feed the dogs before we all went inside to the warm for roast Upland goose with orange sauce and a crate of Chilean Austral beer.

Sam setting off on his mutton chop marathon

Sunset, West Falkland

I landed at Fox Bay and Tony Blake took me up the track to his house at Little Chartres where I was to blood sample some sheep. All went well, the only excitement being when a big Suffolk ram carted Tony from one end of the shearing shed to the other and slammed him against the wall. It was a 'late flight' back to town the next day so I resolved to get up early and do some Sea trout fishing in the Chartres river before breakfast.

I slept lightly with excitement and woke at dawn, the clouds just turning silver on the horizon. I lay in silence for ten minutes or so and then, with the generator off, I dressed and crept downstairs in complete darkness. Quietly I put on all my waterproof gear, my wellies, found my fishing rod and I was out of the door like a poacher of old.

Opposite. Little Chartres

It was freezing outside, I could hear the river running fast but it was still too dark to see. I glanced skywards, the dawn was still appearing in the west. The west, the west, oh foolish boy. I went back inside and sat in an armchair; the kitchen was warm from the stove and pitch black. I had no torch to check my watch, but after a while I noticed the faint, flickering, indicator light from the battery powered answer phone. I stole across to it, held my watch up close, and peered intently as though my life depended on it. 2.15 a.m.! The light outside was merely the moon behind the clouds playing tricks on my fanciful mind. I went back to bed.

When the dawn truly came it was my best morning's trout fishing ever. In two and a quarter hours I caught 15 fish ranging from one and a half to four and a half pounds in weight and I kept five of them for the freezer, enough to keep us fed all winter. I ran back to the farmhouse for fear of being late but, as it turned out, the plane was delayed. There was plenty of time to clean the fish, eat a good cooked breakfast, and laugh with everyone about my early morning foray.

A hundred metres from the house at Little Chartres was a mound of rocks and dirt left from the road building. On top of this, a Red-backed hawk had made its nest and when I visited one spring there were two chicks being cared for. I approached carefully, (Lynn told me how the female had seen off a patrol of Gurkhas a few days previously), and climbed as close as I dare. The hawk eyed me with a piercing stare and then emitted a high pitched warning shriek. I took my picture and left her in peace.

I had gone to Hill Cove to trim a bull's feet and castrate a Tom cat for Tim and Sally, and to check a bitch I'd operated on a few weeks previously for Peter and Shelley Nightingale. Now, in the late afternoon sun I had walked down past the shearing shed, surprising a young Turkey Vulture resting on the fence and who lazily flapped his way up onto the roof.

I went out on the jetty and sat down halfway along, not wanting to disturb the flock of Rock shags perched amongst the white guano on the end. I dangled my legs over the side and looked down into the clear, cold water. On the rocks close to the shore some Crested ducks waddled up and down and the bright scarlet breast of a Military starling shone out from the surrounding yellow gorse.

The bay was as calm as I had ever seen it, the silence was inspiring. When sounds did appear, they were crisp and clear, like single notes. You could feel them, almost see them, so different from the constant background of indiscriminate noise that so often surrounds us. The braying of the Jackass penguins on the tussac island came floating across, I almost cried with the power of emotion I felt inside me. I sat there in the warmth and light, closed my eyes, and did something that Sarah tells me I never do; simply listened.

The tussac island in the bay at Hill Cove

FALKLAND WINTER

We arrived on an RAF Tristar at the end of the worst winter on record, escorted into Mount Pleasant Airport military base by a Tornado fighter-bomber on each wing. Falkland Islands winters, contrary to popular belief, are usually fairly mild affairs, any snow only lying for a day or two and then melting away into the landscape. This year we were told, it had been different, thick snow lying for months at a time with sheep trapped in snow drifts as farmers struggled first to find them, and then release them. Many had died and even the Upland geese had suffered badly.

Luckily, during the next three years we never had a bad winter. True we had some days of heavy snow when snowmen and sledges came alive, but we had day after day of crisp, bright sun, with aching blue skies, that begged you to walk and run along the ice-cold sand at Surf Bay. Such days were invariably calm, the wind blows stronger and more constant in the spring and summer, and wrapped in scarves and fleeces you could imagine that you were on some deserted island in the Caribbean or Pacific, with only the gulls and dolphins for company.

Opposite. Flying to Hill Cove after the storm
Above. Islander landing Hill Cove

Above. Heading for snow storms to the west of Stanley
Below. Port Howard landing strip

It had snowed all night and the wind had blown fiercely. I sat at the airport for more than an hour whilst the pilots waited for the latest weather news. When it came, they decided that it was at least worth a try at getting me over to the West to see an acutely sick dog.

We took off in filtered sunlight, there were snow squalls all around and the mountains to the west of Stanley emanated danger. We stayed low, no more than five hundred feet and large groups of sheep in sheltered spots scattered as we passed overhead. We veered south a little to avoid a heavy snow squall straight ahead.

We came lower still onto Falkland Sound, a wind-whipped chasm of deep grey sea and foam-lashed shores, and then suddenly there were black storms everywhere, with nowhere to escape. I was in the co-pilot's seat and I saw a few stray flakes hit the windscreen and then everything was white, a swirling, whirling shade of white that disconnected you from the outside world. My first thought was to panic but Derek seemed unmoved by it all and so I stayed calm. Time seemed to have no meaning and then we were through, heading towards the coastal hills of West Falkland and a faint glint of sun on the far away mountains.

The landing strip at Port Howard lay smooth and white, the fresh snow dragged us to a shuddering halt. Poor Katie was in a bad way, thin and dehydrated with severe gastro-enteritis. I put her on an intravenous drip and sat with her all that day in the porch where she lay. The next morning I took her to town by plane to continue her treatment and in the next few days she made an uneventful recovery. To her owner's joy, and I think surprise, she was soon winging her way home again.

The storm had passed and now the real pleasure unfolded. We flew to Hill Cove on West Falkland across a gleaming, glistening land of white and blue of every shade, a land of untouched brilliance and delight. Our friend Dae met us at the landing strip with her young daughter Reba. Paul was away killing a bullock she explained.

We were off to stay with them at Shallow Bay, an hour and a half away from the main settlement across bogs and rocky ridges, there were no roads here. We slipped and slid our way along the Sound Ridge in their red 'Rover' with its chunky tractor tyres, and all around the freshness of the scene seemed all the more fine. From the top of Channel Hill we looked down to their little home sat alone and watching out to Keppel Island and Pebble Island beyond, and tears choked up in my eyes. Then, in the far deep distance amidst the snowy landscape and the gathering gloom, we saw Paul homeward bound on his tractor, a massive beef carcass swinging from a great gambrel behind.

Paul prepares the Sunday joint

The view to Pebble Island from the hill above Shallow Bay

The next morning all the snow had gone. Sarah and some of the kids went with Dae to milk the two house cows, the cat, 'Starry-up', tagging along to show off his party trick of catching a spray of warm milk in his mouth squirted straight from the teat. After breakfast we went down onto the beach in front of the house and poked about in rock-pools for fish and crabs. Another of Dae's cats followed us and made half-hearted attempts to hunt the oystercatchers that patrolled the foreshore in flocks of ten or a dozen. Nat and Esme drifted away with Reba and we found them working with serious devotion on decorating a sandcastle with beach-combed artefacts. To me it was art in its most genuine sense, self-expression, pure and simple.

Reba (left), Nat and Esme with sand sculpture

CARCASS ISLAND

For me, Carcass Island is the jewel of the Falklands. It is the most north westerly of the inhabited islands and from the northern tip you can stare out to the deserted Jasons in the middle distance. The owners are Rob and Lorraine McGill. Through the winter Rob lives in Stanley, but in the summer he is out on his island. There, he shears his sheep, milks his cows, and plays host to the thousands of visitors who briefly land from the touring cruise ships, treating them to wonderful cream teas brimming with the home cooking of one of his relatives, 'Aunt'. There are two self-catering holiday cottages and Rob and Aunt give visitors to these the most kindly of welcomes in their big bright kitchen, with mugs of steaming tea and home baked cakes, scones and biscuits dripping with home produced butter and thick, thick cream. We have spent three happy holidays on the island flying in across 'The Saddle' between the Rocky Ridge on one side and the twin peaks of Mount Byng on the other, then down onto the flat grass landing strip beyond. We have never been ready to leave.

To explain the beauty of Carcass is not easy but I will try. Imagine a simple cottage at the top of a wide green track sloping down to a clump of trees and palms with dense yellow flowered gorse all around. Look beyond to the deep blue waters of the bay and the peninsula of land that sweeps round in a huge horseshoe pointing the way to the pale, needle rocks in the distance. Watch how the blueness of the water contrasts with the brown kelp beds that rise and fall with the moving waves, and see the dolphins gently rippling the glistening surface with their games. Listen as the braying sound of the Jackass penguins engulfs you in evening's pinky glow, and the wings of the passing Upland geese caress you with their soft flutterings. All around flit tiny House wrens and Tussac birds, two old horses keep each other company in the fading light. The peace that surrounds you, becomes you, and you wish that the feeling would stay with you forever.

Above: Palms amongst the gorse
Opposite: The view from our holiday cottage, Carcass Island

Nat meets the mare that ran away from Rob

One morning as we sat on the green with the Johnny Rooks begging strips of mutton from us, Rob passed by astride an old bay mare. He gave us his usual cheery smile and wave and disappeared over the hill behind us to bring the cows home for calving. The children watched him go and five minutes later (to their delight), they watched the mare come cantering back, reins and stirrups flapping, no rider in sight. Ten minutes later Rob appeared, plodding along on foot, the same cheery smile on his face. He had got off to open a gate and the mare had seized her chance to break free and head for home. Rob caught her, remounted, and began the day again.

At Elephant Flat we made our way through the tussac grass and out onto the west facing shore. At the high tide mark the kelp was piled thick, wet and slippery, with swarms of tiny flies and sandhoppers which the Tussac birds busied themselves with catching. At the water line, Crested duck and Logger duck paddled, and White-rumped sandpipers rushed back and forth in search of food. A pair of Johnny Rooks followed us along, perching in the crowns of the tussac bogs and then swooping onto the exposed rocks just a few yards in front of us. Kelp geese sat resting and Black-browed albatross cruised and soared on the breeze only feet above the waves.

James spotted them first lying disguised and sleeping on a flat rock shelf surrounded by crisp, dried kelp. As we went closer they stirred and one suddenly sat upright with a half-cocked stare like a Labrador dog whose master had just entered the room. They were young sea lions, probably last year's pups we thought, companions on this

Young sea lions

lonely shore. They watched us for a few minutes and then, sensing I guess that we posed no threat, they settled down once more to their slumbers.

We meanwhile crossed back through the tussac, coming across a patch of open grassland where Antarctic skuas suddenly dived at us. We ran for cover, disturbing a pair of Upland geese and their four goslings who made off with some haste. To our dismay one of the goslings headed in the wrong direction and was soon separated from the others, an easy meal for the skuas as we had already witnessed on several occasions. The children began to cry.

Feeling somewhat to blame for its predicament I raced after it and plucked it up from the grass where it had instinctively crouched. Little Esme cuddled it to her and they all begged me to get it back to its family who by now were entering the sea some eighty yards away. Taking the little life of grey brown down gently in my hands, I walked across to where the other geese were now swimming, thirty yards or so off shore. I placed it carefully in the water and pushed it towards them. It immediately swam back to me; it seemed that I was now its adoptive mother. Once more I pushed it out and it swam in the opposite direction, the waves throwing it back up onto the rocks. I carried it further to a point where the rocks reached out to the ocean and at least it now appeared that the adults were showing some interest in what I was up to. This time it struggled out to sea for a few yards and fortunately made some plaintive whistling noises as it paddled. The goose immediately answered and the two of them rushed towards each other calling all the while. They touched briefly and then the goose led the way back to the gander, the wayward gosling following close behind. I think all of us watching felt an uplifting of the spirit and a sense of relief.

Left. Esme and the gosling
Right. Gentoo colony on the way to Leopard Beach

Above. Upland goose nest
Below. Magellanic oystercatcher nest

The walk to Leopard Beach takes you along a green track with gently sloping dips and gullies, past Magellanic penguin burrows, Upland and Kelp geese on their nests, and dolphins in the bays below.

As you near the point, the sound of the Gentoo colony gradually enters your senses and a little later the smell of them mingles in too, wafted on the gentle breeze. Between their nests and the sea a constant stream of activity, of men in dark suits in twos and threes, hurrying purposefully along the well worn paths.

On the beach itself, a great curving beach of purest white dunes forty feet high, the ducks and penguins loaf and potter. We found a sheltered place warmed by the sun, between rocks and sand grass where the wind couldn't reach and we drank a cold beer and listened to the calming sound of the South Atlantic's song. So still and safe, the children built sand-castles and played in rock pools, suddenly shattered by a three quarter grown bull sea lion who snatched a female Logger duck from the surface of the sea only forty metres in front of us. He tossed her back and forth with a brutality and savagery that was startling and at one point an unlaid egg flew high into the air from her broken body. Her mate meanwhile paddled slowly to the shore but could not resist an occasional backward glance, perhaps in pity or disbelief.

The sea lion soon grew tired of his game and left the torn and lifeless form to float dispiritedly away as easy pickings for the Kelp gulls and sheathbills. He watched us for a few minutes and then swam steadily along the shoreline in search of other sport. Penguins porpoised out of the water in front of him and hit the beach running as they made their way to safety.

The Logger drake sat beside us at the water's edge all day long, and when we returned the next morning he was still there. Whether he was waiting in the hope of his mate's return or because he knew not what else to do we could not say, but his devotion had a sufferance that touched my heart.

The Logger drake who lost his mate to the sea lion

Above. The white sands of Leopard Beach
Left. Gentoo penguin and chicks

Rob had lent us his old Rover and we had driven to near the top of Mount Byng to have a picnic. As we ate our sandwiches we watched the courtship flight of a pair of Peregrine falcons. High in the clear blue sky they mewed noisily to each other, touching momentarily in flight before one would suddenly break away and soar out over a sea awash with Rock shags, King cormorants, and Black-browed albatross.

A female Red-backed hawk dropped down into the crags above us where we assumed it had a nest, and a Johnny Rook landed on a grey outcrop only five yards from where we sat. He rested there, shining eyed and watched us with an interest born of greed for our lunch. We threw him a crust or two and he hopped ungainly to the ground, snatching the morsel in his powerful hooked beak before returning to his perch.

The kids swarmed up and down the rocks, the sun warmed our faces and it was perfect to be alive.

Above. 'Rockhoppers' on Mount Byng
Right. The Johnny Rook that shared our lunch

An Antarctic skua took flight in front of us. It headed directly away for eighty metres, turned in a wide circle gaining height all the while, and came screaming back, the proverbial boomerang. It accelerated as it dropped down to below my head height and then, at the last moment it rose and the rush of wind and the sound of it lashed my face. Time and again it came and then we spotted the fluffy chick in the grass lying motionless and silent. I quickly photographed it, we moved away, and the adult called off its attack.

Above. Antarctic skua
Below. Antarctic skua chick

Below. Looking back to the settlement from the 'standing man'

Kelp geese; the goose following the gander

Pair of Ruddy-headed geese with nesting Magellanic oystercatcher in foreground

One of the simple pleasures of Carcass Island is to sit on the shore just below the settlement and let the world pass by; a world of Kelp geese, Night herons, oystercatchers, Johnny Rooks and much, much more besides. In the trees behind is a heron rookery, untidy, guano stained nests higgledy-piggledy in the branches, the young occupants crouched down inside or perched precariously on the edge whilst the adults hunt for fish in the pools and shallows.

Johnny Rooks and Turkey vultures search the shoreline behind the old fish walls for mullet stranded by the retreating tide, mobbed from time to time by nesting oystercatchers when they approach too close. There are no cats on Carcass and the small nesting birds, House and Grass wrens, Falkland thrushes and Tussac birds, hop and flit at your feet without want or fear. Fishing penguins surface to take breath and then dive again or climb out onto the rocks to take the sun. Dolphins cruise and play in full view with gentle, haunting, charm.

Sometimes when I close my eyes I can imagine that I am there now and an inner smile and warmth spreads across my mind. Carcass Island appears as a magnificent dream; a dream that I think for all of us, for a time at least, came marvellously and wonderfully true.

Above. Black-crowned night heron
Below. Falkland thrush

Above. Blackish oystercatcher on nest
Opposite. Looking across to Byron Heights, West Falkland

AND SO FAREWELL

It was a calm spring day in late November and we headed for a last look at Gypsy Cove, a tiny secluded bay just a few miles from Stanley. The children were happy, thoughts of our homeward trip through Chile and Argentina bubbling in their heads. They ran and jumped their way along the track, kicking up the sand, laughing and giggling. We had come this route countless times in the three years we had lived in Stanley, leaving Bluebell at the wreck of The Lady Elizabeth and then walking across a flat green plain; up the hill; and down the sand and rocks to the footpath that runs along the minefield fence preventing access to the sweeping beach that is York Bay.

Over the stile we went, then up to the tiny tussac plantation where the Jackass have their burrows and from where we once looked down onto the beach to see a sleeping Leopard seal. Another time at this spot, we had seen a hunting sea lion follow a penguin out of the sea up the beach and then to the top of the cliff itself, eventually catching the terrified bird and carrying it back down to the water in its jaws like a trained gun dog.

I thought back to our first Christmas when the twins were only eighteen months old. On that Boxing day we'd carried them to here on our backs and sat down in the shelter of the rocks as the three older boys ran in and out of the sea in the warming sun. The twins had been grizzly and tired, and eventually with much walking up and

Above: The twins asleep at Gypsy Cove, Boxing day 1995
Opposite: On the way to Gypsy Cove

Bluebell takes a breather on the Austral Highway, Southern Chile

down we'd got them to sleep and lain them down on the soft sand in the shadow of the cliffs. They slept there for an hour or more, and whilst we paddled some distance away, a pair of Dolphin gulls alighted close by and pecked hopefully at their brightly coloured jump-suits.

A lot had happened to us in the last three years. We had made some great friends, special friends who had welcomed us into their lives, and we had seen many unique and wondrous things. We were ready to leave but we felt an awful pang, a wrench from this place that we had come to know and love so well. It had been an adventure, yes, a real adventure and the memories we would take with us forever, to be relived and enjoyed again and again.

But now though, we were setting out on another adventure, a great camping journey through Chile and Argentina in Bluebell, back to Brazil to see friends where we had lived ten years before. So we swapped one adventure for another and that eased the parting and we left the Falklands on the crest of a different wave that was to take us westwards, northwards and finally eastwards and all the way home.